Comfort Living. A lifestyle t[hat] [value]s [i]nner priorities and meaning[...]s. [B]alance. A way of living in harmony with [th]e outside world, by being aware of change [a]nd flexible to make adjustments along [th]e way. **Campfires**. Easy but intentional [c]ombinations of objects and routines that [d]raw people in for a sense of well-being, [c]omfort and community. **Treasures**. Anything [o]r anyone that is personally meaningful and [en]courages happiness, contentment, connec-[ti]on or joy. **Bridges**. People, places, objects [a]nd routines that ease connection and flow. [R]ythm. The unique pace of a person's life, [b]ased on inner priorities. **by Christine Eisner**

Table of Contents

Introduction

"*There's no place like home.*"

Dorothy

Remember in "The Wizard of Oz" how Dorothy looked everywhere and asked everyone in her search to find a way back home — only to learn that she herself possessed the answer all along?

In these demanding times, many people are yearning for a way to find more balance and meaning in life. But you don't need to travel far or consult experts to discover the solutions. Happiness begins at home! It is at home where we can find refuge, fun, romance, inspiration and much more. Our surroundings have the power to shape and reflect what matters most to us.

My favorite quote comes from Winston Churchill: *"We shape our dwellings, and afterwards, our dwellings shape us."* Over the past three decades, I have enjoyed working in communications and interior design with the likes of Polo/Ralph Lauren and Sotheby's International Realty, as well as with private clients and design students. I have learned that shaping your dwelling to fit your lifestyle is a satisfying experience available to everyone. You will be surprised at how easily it works!

With simple tools and do-able steps, *Comfort Living* will guide you in creating a home that transforms the way you experience each day. Just as comfort food does more than satisfy hunger, Comfort Living willl realign your surroundings so that they support your priorities and feed your soul.

- If you're searching for your keys in the morning instead of sitting down for breakfast, this book is for you.
- If you envy the cozy nooks you see in catalogs and magazines but don't have a clue about how to create your own, this book is for you.
- If you already enjoy fixing up your home with fabrics and furnishings but wonder if the look reflects who you truly are, this book is for you.
- If you are not able to enjoy your "decorated" home as much as you thought you would, this book is for you.
- If you simply want to make your house more of a home — a place that revives you each day — this book is definitely for you!

Like Dorothy, you already possess the power to make your home a place of refuge and comfort. No big investment of time or money is required. Instead, consider *Comfort Living* an 8-week investment in yourself and those who live with you, with lasting effects.

How To Use This Book

Getting Started

Each chapter in *Comfort Living* will prompt and guide you to reflect on what matters most to you, along with step-by-step tools, exercises and examples that show you how to use these tools in your own home. The last two pages of each chapter offer space to scribble your To Do's and observations and plan for the coming week. The terms in Green are defined on page 70 and 71. At the back of the book there are also pages to develop your Personal Profile, make notes and stay in touch. This approach makes it easy to take action and get results.

Let's get started! Read through the examples below and pick one that appeals to you. Put down this book and follow up right away. Don't wait any longer to give yourself some Comfort Living. You, and those who live with you, deserve it!

Inside Your Front Door

Go take a look at what you see when you first walk through your front door (or your back door or your garage door, if that's how you enter the house). Does it invite you inside and give you permission to leave the world behind? Is it a place of meaning that generates happy feelings? Now look around your home or check closets and drawers for something that you treasure, but have overlooked. Give your special something a place of prominence on a wall or table in your entry. How about adding a vase of flowers or a plant, a doormat or a small rug? Find a tray or bowl to capture your keys, cell phone and sunglasses. Plug a lamp into a light timer — under $5 at the hardware store — and instead of a dark, unwelcoming re-entry, you will return to a cozy nest the next time you cross the threshold.

The Place You Land

Instead of rushing around when you return home, why not take a few minutes to pause and regroup before tackling what needs to be done? Consider where you usually land. Is the chair comfortable? Is there a rug under your feet and a side table to accommodate a cold drink or a cup of tea? Can you reach the newspaper or magazine you want to read? What about reading glasses and a letter opener for the day's mail? Would you like to prop your feet while catching up with a phone call to a friend? Imagine how relaxing it would be to have your favorite music loaded and within arm's reach, so you could hit "play" and enjoy.

Feed Yourself

What's for dinner? Coming home to a table that has been set in advance is so much more welcoming, whether it is on a tray, a counter or the dining table. It doesn't really matter if a meal has been simmering on the stove for hours, pulled from the microwave in a matter of minutes or grabbed from the takeout place on the way home. Try arranging flatware and napkins the night before. It only takes a couple of extra minutes to set out a candle, with matches close at hand, and add placemats or a tablecloth. Then, when you return at the end of the day, you can pretend the butler did it!

The elements of this book should not be mistaken for a crash course in Comfort Living. It is a path to a more balanced way of life that requires small amounts of time and effort, each day. The journey is what counts, and it ideally should involve the people who live with you, even though you might be the one leading the way. An occasional 10-minute conversation at the dinner table or elsewhere may be all it takes to make your family feel part of the process and for you to get a feel for what matters to them. Who knows, they might even become your travelling companions!

Each week's actions are geared to move you forward in a way that is intentional and specific. Plan to spend at least 15 minutes a day, book in hand, in your home — and make use of the weekly calendars to stay on track. A small journal will be a helpful tool for recording positives, negatives, thoughts and To Do's. My companion notebook, *The Comfort Living Journal* is designed for this purpose.

You'll see, with each chapter, each week, you will feel positive change in your home life. It will come, easily and gradually.

Part One: First Steps

Begin with the simple act of pausing to re-examine what makes you happy and relaxed. You will be surprised at how quickly you can bring change to your home by emphasizing your pleasures & treasures, and then clearing away the obstacles that get in their way.

"Home is where we feel at ease, where we belong, where we can create surroundings that reflect our tastes and pleasures."

Sir Terence Conran

WEEK 1

Looking Inward:
Treasures & Obstacles

Homes should be a haven for the people who live in them, not just a display for "company."

With comfort and convenience as your priorities, it's easier to improve your lifestyle than you think— if you have the right tools. The first step on the path to Comfort Living is taking stock of what matters to you.

You'll find questions at the end of this chapter to prompt your thinking about your lifestyle priorities, including your home and your possessions as well as your routines and relationships. Once you've focused awareness on the most valued aspects of your life, they become the stepping stones to creating your Comfort Lifestyle.

Your Treasures & Obstacles

These next exercises will help you become more aware of the activities, routines and Rhythms that make up who you are, how you set up your surroundings and how you live your life. This is not about passing judgement on your choices or comparing your home to glossy magazine covers. Many people assume that having the home they want requires major expenditures on furnishings or renovations. In fact, you may be surprised to discover how much satisfaction comes from small moments of joy tucked into each day.

A 2007 University of Nottingham study of lottery jackpot winners, titled "Happiness Comes Cheap — Even for Millionaires," documented that even for people who can afford whatever they want, it's the simple, cost-free pleasures that lead to happiness. The study reported, "Happy people — whether they are lottery jackpot winners or not — like long baths, going swimming, playing games and enjoying their hobby. It appears that spending time relaxing is the secret to a happy life. Cost-free pleasures are the ones that make the difference — even when you can afford anything that you want."

Tuning In To Your Treasures & Obstacles

Here's where you become more attuned to your Treasures, those experiences that lift your spirits, as well as your Obstacles, the ones that weigh you down. With a clearer picture in mind, the idea is to turn up the volume on the positives, while turning it down on the negatives that get in the way. Hopefully, the examples that follow will prompt some ideas for when you start tuning in to your own.

Treasures

Think about times when you feel really contented, satisfied, inspired and happy. Most likely, these are moments you cherish. These are what I call Treasures — experiences, people, places and objects that are uniquely meaningful.

Here are some to consider:

- Treating yourself (or someone else) to a morning in bed
- Feeling the satisfaction of getting To Do's done
- Coming home and changing into comfy clothes
- Enjoying sunlight on a terrace or through a window
- Savoring a home-cooked meal on your favorite china
- Cozying up with a good book, a pet or someone you love
- Baking cookies to share

Obstacles

Obstacles make us appreciate Treasures even more. They are those interactions with people, possessions and places that stir up feelings of discomfort, stress, depression or anger. Obstacles interrupt the flow of day-to-day living.

So, what are your Obstacles? Here are some to consider:

- Having to constantly sift through "stuff" to find what you need
- Trying to make your bed daily, in spite of an overflow of pillows and shams
- Rushing out of the house and realizing that you forgot your keys
- Working at a desk piled high with papers, bills and unopened mail
- Coming home to dirty dishes in the sink
- Feeling like there's nowhere at home to relax — except maybe in front of the TV or computer

This week you will be starting your own lists. Of course, your Treasures and Obstacles are bound to change over time. Every so often, monthly or seasonally, make a point of updating them. That way, you can stay tuned into the elements that influence your Comfort Life.

EXERCISE / Your Comfort Home, In Your Own Words

Think about how you want to feel when you are at home. Without the distraction of colors, styles or stylized photographs, circle your words, the ones that describe your Comfort Home:

CALM	COMFORTABLE	USEFUL	NEAT	AIRY	HUMBLE
ORGANIZED	INSPIRATIONAL	COZY	FRIENDLY	TRADITIONAL	QUIET
COOL	IMPRESSIVE	BUSY	GLITZY	STIMULATING	PRETTY
LIVED-IN	SERENE	CASUAL	WHIMSICAL	HIGH-TECH	CLUTTERED
EDGY	SIMPLE	NATURAL	EFFICIENT	SLEEK	GREEN
VINTAGE	GLAMOROUS	VIBRANT	UNIQUE	UNPREDICTABLE	SPORTY
FEMININE	MASCULINE	COMPACT	ROMANTIC	ARTSY	RETRO
WACKY	FASHIONABLE	SUBDUED	COLORFUL	PRIVATE	CASUAL

Now cross out the words that don't appeal to you.

Finally, rewrite your Comfort Home Words here, along with any others that come to mind:

_____   _____   _____   _____

_____   _____   _____   _____

_____   _____   _____   _____

Before you move on to the next page, and with your chosen words in mind, take a closer look at the areas of your home that you enjoy most. Ask yourself:

- What makes them appealing?

- Do they reflect some of your Comfort Home Words?

- Do your treasured experiences tend to take place in those areas?

- What areas or rooms do you wish you used more?

- What might make them more inviting? How can they become Treasures?

You may not realize it, but in just these few pages, you have looked inward and begun to articulate your Lifestyle Priorities, those elements of living that hold the most meaning for you and those who live with you. Keep these priorities in mind as you turn the page, and you will be moving forward on the path to Comfort Living!

Week One / To Do's

Become more aware of your Treasures and Obstacles as you go through this week. Look inward, realizing that the greener grass might be right under your feet.

ACTIONS

- Schedule at least 15 minutes each day of this week to focus on Treasures and Obstacles. Use the weekly planner on page 21.
- Keep a running list of your Treasures and Obstacles.
- Start a journal. If you are taking notes in *The Comfort Living Journal*, use the sections designated for Treasures and Obstacles.
- Apply what you learned in the Introduction to make any immediate improvements that come to mind.
- At the end of the week, take 15 minutes to look over your Treasures and Obstacles lists. Circle the best of your Treasures and write them below. Do the same with your Comfort Home Words on page 17.

These two groups of words will become your Lifestyle Priorities.

LIFESTYLE PRIORITIES =

TOP TREASURES   +   COMFORT HOME WORDS

OBSERVATIONS

- Think about why the items on your Treasures list are important to you. Write down your thoughts.

- Does your home reflect your Lifestyle Priorities? What changes would you like to see happen?

Identify your Lifestyle Priorities by taking stock of your
Treasures and how you want to feel when you are at home.

week 1

M

T

W

T

F

S

S

WEEK 2

Streamlining:
Change for the Better

Sometimes just getting through a day can feel like running a marathon in ski boots. Inundated by paperwork, phone calls, text messages, tweets and e-mail, repairs, bills and more, we often feel overwhelmed by Obstacles that make "the good life" seem like a pipedream. Then there are those dream days when everything goes our way, and it's like gliding through twists and turns on a fast set of skis.

While you can't make the necessary tasks of everyday life vanish into thin air, the right tools can make coping with them much easier. Streamlining is one of those tools.

Streamlining is the ongoing process of eliminating or minimizing the Obstacles that get in the way of living well. Streamlining will allow your Treasures to command more attention and your physical surroundings to become invitations to relax and enjoy.

Streamlining is one of the key tools for Comfort Living. The goal is not to do a one-time cleanout, but to make it a regular routine to clear the way for positive change. For many of us, this is no easy task, and enlisting the aid of a professional organizer or a hyper-organized buddy can make the difference between fight or flight!

The Essentials of Home Tending

Whether you live in a single room, an apartment, or a 10-bedroom house, home-tending energizes your surroundings and keeps you connected to your home. Simply put:

- If you open it, close it
- If you put it down, pick it up
- If you take it off, hang it up
- If you mess it up, clean it up
- If you take it out, put it back

I will talk more about bringing positive routines into your life, but keep in mind that making a habit of home-tending is where Comfort Living begins. You will be clearing a path that makes it easier to enjoy the small pleasures and relaxing moments that make a good life.

Think of Streamlining as taking stock and sorting through possessions to minimize distractions. Take time to think, but not too much time — otherwise you run the risk of keeping everything. By the way, there is no "I'll deal with it later" option in the four phases of Streamling!

- **PRESERVE / HONOR** — Things that are "keepers" need to be treated with respect and care. If repairs are needed, get them done. Then place them so they play a greater role in your day-to-day.

- **PUT AWAY / STORE** — Establish homes for necessities — and use them. Whether they go in the attic, in a cabinet, on a hook or shelf, remember that not everything needs to be in plain sight.

- **GIVE AWAY / SELL** — You know what they say, one man's trash is another man's Treasure. So go create some Treasures by making a gift of your trash.

- **RECYCLE / THROW AWAY** — If you don't need it, get rid of it! Whenever possible, make the extra effort to recycle.

The ToolBox below assures that the task will be quicker and easier.

Your ToolBox for Streamlining

- trash cans, trash bags, boxes, packing tape, recycling bins
- label-maker, permanent markers
- storage containers, drawers, shelves, bookends, baskets, trays, bowls, hooks, cabinets, closets, file cabinets
- clutter-phobic friends and/or professional organizers (www.napo.net)
- FreeCycle.com - to make your trash someone else's Treasure
- dropoff locations and telephone numbers for donation pick-ups
- electrical cord organizers, extension cords, 3-way plugs
- *The Comfort Living Journal* or a notebook for jotting down your actions and observations

---

Just a few hours of Streamlining on a regular basis will yield huge payoffs in all aspects of your life. By making a commitment to your surroundings, you will be richly rewarded with reduced stress and more time for what you enjoy most.

Exercise / Quick Fix Lessons from a Catalog

There are lessons to be learned in the pages of any home catalog. Pick one up and read on.

As you flip the pages, notice the objects that are not for sale. Fresh flowers, artwork, framed photographs, painted walls and lighting are the tools of the trade that make products more appealing. Every detail is carefully considered long before you open your mailbox or add something to your on-line shopping cart.

Clutter Distracts

In any catalog worth its salt, you will see an absence of clutter. Arbitrary "stuff" only serves as a distraction. Same with your personal surroundings, the less that gets in the way, the easier it is to focus on the essentials.

The Forces of Nature

Unless yours is a gardening catalog, the plants and flowers you see are important props. Count on nature having a presence from the first page to the last. A basket of fresh fruit on a countertop, a pot of narcissus on a sofa table, a crystal bowl of shells or river stones on a shelf, a vase of fresh tulips on a mantle, or even a single rose on a bathroom vanity is all that's needed. These ideas are not very complicated, yet the power of each one is surprising in a catalog — and even more in a home setting.

Lighting is Key

Look at the use of light in your catalog. Lighting invariably warms up spaces and brings objects and people to life. Windows and window treatments can maximize sunlight, and artificial lighting picks up where the sun leaves off. Consider the effects of a hanging fixture casting a pool of light on a dinner table, a set of swing-arm lamps flanking a bed (all the more space to showcase products on the night tables!) or outdoor pathway lights leading to a front door. Lighting is an often overlooked tool, but it is one of the quickest and easiest ways to positively impact space.

Color Counts

Check out how each photograph puts color to work. Some examples: a breakfast nook painted in a honey-vanilla hue captures the morning sun; all-white bedrooms with accents in blues and greens feel crisp and inviting; black and ivory faux-painted floors or dark wood-paneled walls reinforce the drama of an entry, living room or library. In your own spaces, whether you use high-end specialty paints or whatever is on sale at your local hardware store, color counts in a BIG way.

The bottom line is to keep in mind that details can enrich living environments. Lamps can really cozy up a seating area, but don't introduce just any lamp. Consider the options before buying to be sure the one you take home reflects your Lifestyle Priorities.

In a few words, be intentional about the choices you make and make the details work for you... just like the pros do!

Week Two / To Do's

Discover the benefits of Streamlining. Emphasize your Treasures by removing or minimizing Obstacles.

ACTIONS

- Right now, look around your home and identify at least 3 objects you do not want to keep or preserve because you no longer use or need them. Now deal with them. Think: preserve / honor, put away /store, give away / sell, recycle / throw away.
- Schedule at least 15 minutes each day this week for Streamlining. Create your ToolBox and identify 3 areas that need taming — a junky kitchen drawer, a tangle of cords at your desk, a crowded coat closet, your cluttered desktop, a chaotic garage. Make a list of tools that might help and put it to work.
- This week, visit an organizing store or website such as Organize.com for products to add to your ToolBox.
- Remember to record what you accomplish each day by jotting down a few notes on the opposite page.

OBSERVATIONS

- Look over your notes from Week 1. How does your home feel now?

- Which Streamlining routines work for you? Once a week? Once a month? Be realistic.

> Streamlining happens when you remove Obstacles that get in the way so you can emphasize what matters most to you and those who live with you.

week 2

M

T

W

T

F

S

S

Part Two: Guiding Lights

Comfort Living is personal, and that's just the way it should be. The light that guides you comes from within, gently showing you the path to a way of life that encourages your own unique lifestyle. It's up to you to listen to yourself and then set your course accordingly. Look inward first and then focus on creating experiences, rather than appearances.

"An interior is the natural projection of the soul."

Coco Chanel

WEEK 3

Introducing Campfires:
Centers of Energy That Attract

Picture this: You arrive home after a crazy day, welcomed by a warmly lit entry, the table set for dinner, candles ready to light and just minutes from a sit-down dinner.

Hold on a minute! You don't have a guardian angel or a full-time housekeeper. So how do you get to live like this? By creating Comfort Living Campfires.

Unlike the logs-and-sticks variety, Campfires are combinations of places, objects, routines, people and even animals that create a sense of well-being, comfort and community. In earlier days and in nomadic cultures, Campfires were a necessity for survival. Today, they are just as important, but on a deeper level, because they strengthen the connection between people and their surroundings.

Ever so gently, Campfires draw you into their glow, just as the sun entices the heads of sunflowers to follow its arc throughout the day. But instead of being something to look at, as you would a focal point, these Campfires are to be experienced.

Here are some examples of Campfires that you might create:

Reading Campfires for Parent and Child

Reading Campfires start with a lamp, a comfortable chair, and some books. With the added comfort of a lap blanket and a furry friend, you and your child will look forward to cozying up together.

Mealtime Campfires

Instead of a stand-up dinner at the kitchen counter or in front of an open refrigerator, why not try creating a more satisfying mealtime Campfire? Microwave and take-out meals really do taste better when they are eaten on a plate. As you learned in the Introduction, 5 minutes in advance can put the "sit-down" back into dinner. If you are dining solo, a tray pre-set for one assures a nice meal, whether it is at the table, in front of the TV or in bed.

Morning Campfires

Like it or not, getting up early is a fact of life for most of us. Instead of emerging into a dark hallway, wouldn't it be nice to be greeted by a lamp on a side table or at the base of a stairway? With a light timer set to turn on before you get up and go off after you head out for the day, this Campfire practically tends itself.

Campfires for Hanging Out

Not all hang-out areas are created equal. Some of the best Campfire tools are rugs and lamps because they create intimacy. With a lamp on a side table illuminating a few Treasures, a rug underfoot and some music in the background, any sitting area can become a Campfire that says "Relax!"

Workplace Campfires

Get the job done while enjoying the process with a comfortable place to stand or sit, a clear work surface, good lighting and a decent organizing system. Simple, feel-good additions include open windows, colors that inspire, your favorite music and some framed family photographs or art.

Sofa Talk

Sitting areas that earn their keep are those that are physically inviting. Take a minute and put this book down. Check out the distance between your sofa and your coffee table. If it's less than 18 inches, sitting down might be a bit of a squeeze. If it's over 20 inches, then you probably have to get up to reach that magazine or cup of tea. If no table-top surface exists, then you might want to consider one so that your Campfire for hanging out can burn brighter. Could this be a reason why other areas of your home get more use?

"Good Night" Campfires

That same lamp at the base of the stairs — the one that said "good morning" — can also say "good night." Set to turn on again at dusk and turn off a few hours later, this Campfire has the final say when it comes to "lights out."

Take a look back at pages 9 & 10 to review the Campfires that provide:

- A welcome home just inside your door
- A place to land before evening obligations arise
- A sit-down meal that hits the spot

Week Three / To Do's

Look at your spaces and gather your thoughts on how Campfires might contribute to your Comfort Lifestyle. This week is purely for observation and reflection.

ACTIONS

- Right now, take 10 minutes for a quick walk-through of your home, inside and out. Write down at least 3 locations that would benefit from Campfires.

- Schedule at least 15 minutes a day to spend in these areas. Take some notes on how these spaces are, or aren't, being used. How do you want these spaces to feel? How can you make them irresistable?

- Each day use your 15 minutes to observe and plan. Think about how your Campfires can reinforce your Lifestyle Priorities. Start a list of To Do's and remember to include the four phases of Stream-lining. Be specific — but hold off on making any changes until next week.

OBSERVATIONS

- Think about the centers of energy that exist in your home now. Where are they? What behaviors do they encourage?

- How do you want your Campfires to improve the way you live in your home?

> Life is about experiences, not appearances. Campfires encourage experiences to happen, easily and naturally.

week 3

M

T

W

T

F

S

S

Creating Your Own Campfires: Warmth, Energy & Comfort

In the same way that you feel content and rejuvenated in front of a crackling fire, you can recreate that same relaxing glow where you live and work. With a few practical tools and a bit of know-how, building Comfort Living Campfires is easy. Even better, most of what you need is already there for the taking.

A favorite armchair … a chicken roasting in the oven … a pet curled up on a sunny window seat … an upcoming holiday or family occasion … some recent photographs. Each of these is kindling for a Campfire that can transform your house into a home, your home into a nest.

Holiday gatherings are some of the most obvious Campfires. A Thanksgiving table dressed up for the occasion is an invitation to kids and adults to come together. Almost magically, the distractions of ordinary life fade away, giving center stage to meaningful traditions and special people.

Campfire Building Basics

Campfires don't require a lot of time or money. They don't need to be elaborate or perfect. They just need to support the way you want to live. They can be gentle — or totally outrageous. What's important is that they feel right for you and bring your Treasures to the forefront of your life. Here's how to build your own:

Take Stock of Your Space

- Envision your Campfire. Consider the impact of lighting, color, texture, technology and layout. Take notes or make a sketch — whatever captures your thoughts. Or simply dive in!
- Streamline first by sorting out the Obstacles, big or small, to clear a spot for your Campfire.
- Start a To Do list for you or a helper. Include things like making repairs, framing photographs and moving heavy furniture.

Gather Up Your Materials

- Check out the Campfires ToolBox on page 38. Then take a look around your home for your kindling. Be aware that each element you choose should enhance your Campfire's glow. If it doesn't have a purpose, functional, aesthetic or otherwise, steer clear. Clutter only distracts.
- Keep tangible objects in mind, like tabletop surfaces, personal tokens, lamps, light bulbs and rugs. Remember intangibles as well, like sunlight and shade, breezes, scents and music.
- If you get stuck, refer back to the Campfires ToolBox and Chapter 3 for more ideas.

Arrange

- As with logs-and-sticks Campfires, arrangement matters. Be intentional about how you place your Campfire kindling, so it feels right for you.
- Make adjustments as you go. Enlist the aid of hooks, trays, shelves, and baskets to honor Treasures and minimize Obstacles. Sensible spacing of furniture can improve flow. If a short electrical cord prevents a lamp from sitting on a side table, an extension cord, not a new lamp, is the answer. If the lighting is too

dim, maybe a new light bulb or a lighter lampshade will do the trick. For color changes, a can of spray paint can work miracles!

- Now place yourself in your Campfire and think about what else might allow it to glow even more.

Tend

- Campfires are not vignettes or displays. Allow yourself to be drawn to their energy and luxuriate in the intimacy they create.
- Bring Campfires into your daily routines. For a socializing Campfire, light a fire and turn on some music. For a bedtime story Campfire, locate it in a bedroom and factor in a few extra minutes for reading before "lights out."
- Unless you tend them, Comfort Living Campfires will fade away. Allow your campfires to evolve with

your needs and wants. Water plants, update photographs in picture frames, set out a bowl of fruit, use light switches and dimmers and open up the windows.

- While you're at it, unfold that lap blanket, sink into those throw pillows and meander through the coffee table books. The same goes with the "good" china and your grandmother's silver service. These aren't props. They are meant to be part of your present, not saved for the future.

EXERCISE / Campfire Considerations

As you begin creating your own Campfires, whether you are a family of one or a family of eight, take a few minutes to answer these questions. If you live with others, make a point of involving them. A 15-minute conversation may be all you need.

THINK ABOUT	YOU	YOUR PARTNER	YOUR CHILDREN, ROOMMATES, ETC.
What kind of Campfires do you want to create? Where will they be?			
How do you want your Campfires to make you feel?			
What Treasures will add deeper meaning to your Campfires?			
What tools will you use?			
How can you make them more inviting? More functional?			
How will you tend them?			

Your ToolBox for Campfires

TREASURES / photographs, art, mementos, collections, music, gifts, found objects, books, family heirlooms, spiritual symbols, favorite colors, textures, flowers, food, retreats, pets, people

ELEMENTS TO CREATE UNITY OR ORDER / trays, baskets, vases, bowls, decorative mats, shelves, picture frames, albums, scrapbooks

SOFT STUFF / cashmere, velvet, brushed cotton, throw blankets and pillows, robes, a favorite sweatshirt or pair of jeans or slippers

NATURE / views, plants, flowers, fruit, water features, outdoor furnishings, windows, bird feeders, gardens, windowboxes, farm stands, sunsets

COLORS AND TEXTURES / naturals, brights, neutrals, pales, distressed, hand-hewn, beveled, honed, polished, stained

SOUNDS / wind chimes, music, breezes, fountains, birdcalls, falling water, purring

LIGHTING ELEMENTS / sunlight, candles, fireplaces and fire pits, firewood, matches, lamps, dimmers, light timers, night lights, extension cords, outdoor lighting

FURNISHINGS / sofas and armchairs, tabletop surfaces, rugs and runners, rug pads, lamps, shelves, cabinets, day beds, recliners, rocking chairs, umbrellas, awnings

ACTIVITIES / reading materials, musical instruments, games, needlework, journals, edibles, sports equipment, toys, movies, crafts, puzzles, cooking

TABLEWARE / placemats, napkins, napkin rings, favorite foods, salt and pepper, trays, dishes, glassware, flatware

TECHNOLOGY / phones, audio systems, i-pods, CD changers, TVs, computers, remotes, radio pre-sets

Week Four / To Do's

Now it's your turn to build your own Campfires. Start with one for mealtimes and go from there.

ACTIONS

- Right now, spend 5-10 minutes to create an easy mealtime Campfire.
- Schedule at least 15 minutes each day of this week. Each day, use your time to bring to life the Campfires that you envisioned in Week 3. Think about you how you want to feel, what you want to see and what you want to have within arm's reach.
- Make a point of tending your Campfires by simply experiencing them. Jot down some notes or make adjustments to allow them to burn brighter. (A gentle reminder: Take care of your To Do list as well.)

OBSERVATIONS

- How has your home changed as a result of your Campfires?

- What other areas might benefit from Campfires?

When you use Campfires to enrich your home, you are being intentional about shaping the experiences of daily living.

week 4

M

T

W

T

F

S

S

Part Three: Little Things

Birthdays mark the passage of an entire year as if, from one day to the next, we become 365 entire days older. The irony is that life is not lived in years. Lives are shaped by minutes, hours, sunrises and sunsets. The way we choose to live those fractions of time makes us who we are and influences who we will become. The idea is to live fully in the present, while honoring the past and making way for the future.

"Have nothing in your house that you do not know to be useful,
or believe to be beautiful."

William Morris

WEEK 5

Adding Meaning to Everday Objects: Bridges & Echoes

In the world of Comfort Living, something as ordinary as an apple can become much more. Depending on how you look at them, apples can become Bridges to other places and times. Comfort Living Bridges encourage easy flow and connection. Echoes are one particular type of Bridge that brings the past into the present. Like a favorite song or comfort food, the messages of Echoes reach below the surface.

Suppose that you decide to get healthier by eating more fruit. So you go to the grocery store, buy some apples and stick them in the fridge. Goal accomplished, right? Probably not. More likely, you will still find them there one week later, and one week older. On the other hand, five minutes of putting some Bridges and Echoes in place might make the difference between rotten and eaten.

An Apple as a Bridge and an Echo

As a Bridge

Bridges are about ease and flow. Imagine getting home and washing those same apples and placing a basketful on the kitchen counter. With those two small gestures, you have created a Bridge that makes "eating healthy" more likely to happen. Now when you walk into the kitchen, you'll be lured by the apples instead of distracted by the snack drawer. Job done!

As an Echo

Apples may not be among your Treasures, though they might be an Echo of something or someone special. Perhaps they are reminders of the pies served each Thanksgiving when you were growing up or the holiday visits to a favorite uncle's orchard. Whatever the case, when deeper meanings are linked to everyday objects, they create Echoes that add depth to day-to-day living.

Bridges

A Bridge can be a person, place, thing or even a routine. Bridges create connection or continuity. A fabric or color that allows a plaid sofa to work with a flowered armchair is a Bridge. Picture a breezeway linking a garage to a house, or even a doormat at a front door. Both of these ease the transition from one place to another. When Bridges exist, Obstacles are minimized, spaces are enjoyed and life becomes less stressful.

PICTURE THESE SETTINGS:

- An upstairs hall with carpeting underfoot and a series of framed photographs is a Bridge that unifies this more private region of a home. With a bare floor and walls, the feeling of connection and intimacy would be lost.

- A wood-paneled den with cozy seating, bookshelves and ample lamplight is a Bridge to relaxation and reading. If the chairs aren't comfortable or the lighting is poor, readers won't bother to linger.

- The colors in a rug, repeated in adjoining rooms, encourage flow from one room to another.

- A bedroom with French doors open-opening onto a balcony is a

Bridge leading to the outdoors. If there was only a window, the Bridge wouldn't be half as sturdy.

- A drawer for placemats and napkins situated close to the dining table is a Bridge to sit-down dinners. If these items are accessible, setting the table is easier and meals become more enjoyable.

- A decorative tassel on the outside of a powder room doorknob lets people know that it isn't the coat closet!

- At night, a lit and landscaped walkway leading to an illuminated front door is a Bridge that signals "Come in."

Your ToolBox for Bridges

PATHWAYS / furniture spacing, hallway widths, runners, stepping stones

OPENINGS TO OTHER SPACES / doors, glass-paned doors like French and sliding doors, archways, windows, skylights, breezeways

LIGHT / sunlight, candles/matches, fires/logs, lamps, light timers, nightlights, ceiling lights, sconces, outdoor lighting

SHADE / window treatments, porches, awnings, umbrellas, trellises, arbors, trees

SOFT STUFF / music, throws, pillows, blankets, robes, loungewear, slippers

USER-FRIENDLY FLOOR COVERINGS / doormats, rugs, runners, carpeting, stone, wood, tile

SIGNS / obvious or subtle

COLOR / paint, stain, dye, fabrics, wall-coverings

OUTDOOR ROOMS / balconies, terraces, courtyards, barbecue pits

SURFACES FOR EASY ACCESS / side tables, coffee tables, sofa tables, ottomans, tray tables

PLACES TO KEEP TREASURES IN VIEW, BUT OUT OF THE WAY / shelves, mantles, hooks, walls

TABLETOP / placemats, flatware, napkins, trays

NATURE / potted plants, landscaping, outdoor furnishings, grills, bicycles, basketball hoops

Echoes

Consider how much louder a car horn sounds in a tunnel than one heard on the street. When objects or other elements become Echoes of special experiences, they have the power to transport you across time and space. The first notes of a favorite song or the aroma of a comfort food are Echoes.

Echoes bring deeper meaning to everyday objects. They might arise from a photograph, a wedding dress, an antique armchair or from family rituals. By placing these elements where you and others can readily appreciate them, the stories they represent resonate more fully.

Two Real-Life Echoes

TRAVEL
A pair of Adirondack chairs by a front door is the first thing you see as you arrive at the home of our friends. They are a year-round Echo of summers in Martha's Vineyard. Every time I see them, they remind me of good times in the Adirondacks with my own friends, years ago.

COMFORT FOOD
Comfort foods are personal Echoes. My mother's recipe for spaghetti is one of my family's comfort foods. I usually make it when we could use a soothing end to a busy day. When the kids were little, I renamed it "Grammy's Spaghetti." For them, it's an Echo of their grandmother; for me, it brings back a flood of childhood memories.

LISTEN TO THESE ECHOES:

- Late at night, the chiming of an inherited grandfather clock can Echo a childhood home.

- On a kitchen counter, a digital frame with family photographs scrolling by is an Echo of treasured people and memories.

- In the den or office of a successful executive, diplomas, plaques, photographs and other mementos are Echoes of an illustrious career.

- In a bathroom, the use of a certain kind of tile, fabric or soaps can Echo a favorite retreat or vacation home.

- On a coffee table, a single feather or a box of dried rose petals can be an Echo of a gesture of love.

- On a wall, framed artwork of grown children is an Echo that brings warmth and comfort to empty-nesters.

- In a courtyard, falling petals from a cherry blossom tree each spring might Echo a special occasion, like the birth of a baby.

Your ToolBox for Echoes

PASSED-DOWN POSSESSIONS / furnishings, art, jewelry, photographs, clothing

MEMENTOS / travel tickets, restaurant menus, programs, matchbooks

FAVORITES / colors, songs, poems, scents, textures, flowers, plants

FOUND OBJECTS / shells, stones, pine cones

ART / fine art, folk art, posters, childhood crafts

SHOPS / flea markets, vintage stores, antique shops, estate sales

NAMES / passed-down family names, nicknames, titles

PRINTED MATTER / yearbooks, photo albums, baby books, letters, doodles, books

The purpose of Bridges is to ease transitions. In the case of Echoes, the transitions are emotional. Almost anything can create a sense of connection. It is the meaning you assign to something that makes it so much more significant.

Week Five / To Do's

Think about your home as a place where the past, present and future can co-exist in harmony.

ACTIONS

- Schedule 15 minutes each day this week. Right now, walk through your home. As you go, form two lists. On the first, list any blocked areas that might benefit from Bridges. On the second, list any austere spaces, where Echoes might make them more intimate and personal.

- On the next day, use your time to look at your lists and this week's ToolBoxes. Jot down any Bridge and Echo tools that might be useful. Think about the obstacles that are in the way as well as the special memories, people and experiences you want to highlight.

- For the rest of the week, build some Bridges and create some Echoes. Each day, spend time experiencing the journey of your more fluid environment.

OBSERVATIONS

- How does the addition of Bridges and Echoes affect your surroundings? How do they make you feel? What are their messages?

- What changes are you experiencing in your home?

When you make use of Bridges, Campfires become more accessible.

week 5

M

T

W

T

F

S

S

WEEK 6

Balancing Chaos with Predictability:
Routines & Rhythms

Whether your home is a dorm room, a studio apartment or an 8-bedroom house, your daily, monthly and annual routines make up the Rhythm that is unique to your lifestyle. Washing dishes and paying bills may not be life-changing events, but they can counterbalance chaos, fatigue and stress.

Imagine introducing little details that transform routines into Campfires. Take dishwashing as an example. With the lights low, music playing and scented hand lotion for afterwards, the task of washing dishes becomes a lot more pleasant — and you still end up with clean dishes.

Which Routine is for You ?

Bright lights, a quick, shower, a scrap of soap, a still-damp towel grabbed off the floor, a pair of pants from the laundry basket … all part of the race out the door, energy bar in hand.

— vs. —

Lights dimmed, an unrushed, hot shower, scented soap, thick, all-cotton towels on a nearby hook, topped off with a cup of coffee in your robe and slippers before getting dressed for work.

Here are some other examples of everyday routines that can counterbalance the not-so-good things in life:

Home Tending Routines

Every month, take note of what needs cleaning, repairing and Streamlining, and then address these To Do's individually. Dealing with a small leak when it occurs is easier than coping with the resulting mildew and rotted wood a few months down the road.

Work Routines

Whether your workspace is a home office, a laundry room, a garage workshop or all three, predictable routines make work more productive and satisfying. Does it take too long to get situated every time you enter your workspace? Are your systems working for you?

R & R Routines

Encourage fun and down-time on a regular basis. A deck of cards and a Scrabble game in a drawer by the kitchen table makes R & R more likely to happen. A comfortable daybed on a screened-in porch invites a nap. An afternoon cup of tea or some music is an extra nudge in the right direction.

Traditions

Traditions are extra-special, V.I.P. routines. Though some are widespread — like singing "Happy Birthday" or serving turkey on Thanksgiving — others only exist in a

Transforming 2 Daily Routines

BRUSHING TEETH

Every day starts and ends with this basic routine. These quick fixes might work for you:

- Streamlining your vanity top or medicine cabinet
- Adding a bud vase with a flower or some framed photos beside the sink or on the wall
- Posting the week's schedule or a favorite quote for easy viewing
- Sprucing up the bathroom with a new shower curtain, towels, or a fresh coat of paint
- Cleaning the windows to let the sun shine in

YOUR *COMFORT LIVING* JOURNEY

Enhance your routine of travelling through this book by:

- Returning to the same place in your house each day
- Silencing your phone and yourself before opening your book
- Enlisting a friend or two to join you for a collaborative *Comfort Living* experience
- Carrying your journal with you to capture thoughts as they arise

A MEALTIME ROUTINE

Growing up in the Northeast, my family sat down to dinner at 6 o'clock, for better or for worse. A prayer was said, which was as much a blessing as it was a few seconds of quiet time for my mother. For most of the year, we ate indoors, almost always with lit candles on the dining table. Each spring, we relocated to the covered terrace and enjoyed casual menus and fresh air.

We may not have realized it, but my mother's dinner routine was a predictable and comforting Rhythm in our lives. It was a well-tended Campfire designed to reel us in and bring us together as a family at the end of each day.

single household. Either way, they occupy a place of honor. Use these rituals to inspire more frequent routines. For example, where is it written that breakfast in bed is only for Mother's day? Why not make it happen one Sunday a month — even if you aren't a mom?

Making Routines a Reality

Especially when you live with others, but even if you are on your own, communication helps. Make use of basic tools like calendars, alarm clocks, timers, bulletin boards and notepads. These can be reminders to create and enjoy the benefits of routines.

Making routines a reality isn't always easy. In the beginning you might need to consciously schedule time for them, but you will find that the ones that really suit you will work their way into your life.

A Word About Balance

We hear a lot about balance these days. In *Comfort Living*, Balance is about flexibility and change. It is not about hitting the bull's eye on a target and then being "done." Isaac Newton's law of gravity sums it up, "What goes up must come down."

Like two people on a see-saw, Balance means creating momentary resting places, and then as situations change, adjusting accordingly. Balance is a way of living with ease in a changing world.

Favorite Traditions – Candles and Cakes

Candles have always played a prominent role in my family's traditions. Candles at the dinner table, candles on a freshly-cut spruce tree during the holidays, and of course, candles on birthday cakes. For me, special occasions simply would not be the same without them.

An extra-special birthday tradition that is now moving into its third generation in my family occurs on 18th and 30th birthdays. In our home, during the course of two or three days, I bake an elaborate Swiss cake, a Zuger Kirschtorte. Though it doesn't look as pretty as the ones found in Swiss bakeries, every time one of these rites of passage comes around, candles are lit, memories surface and stories are told and retold.

What are some of your routines and special traditions? How might you add more meaning to them?

Week Six / To Do's

Use Treasures, Campfires, Bridges and Echoes to enrich your routines for a Rhythm that is uniquely yours.

ACTIONS

- Schedule at least 15 minutes each day this week. Then make a list of at least 3 routines that you want to create or improve upon.
- Today pick a single routine from your list to focus on this week. Ask yourself: Where in your home does it take place? What changes can make it more meaningful or enjoyable? What tools can you use?
- Record your ideas and make changes to your space. Then schedule this routine into the weekly planner on the opposite page as well as on your personal calendar.
- Each day for the rest of the week, follow your new routine. Take notes on how it makes you feel. If time allows, try modifying another routine.

OBSERVATIONS

- How did the changes to your physical spaces affect your routine? How have they affected your personal Rhythm?

- What other routines do you want to bring into your life more fully? What about longer-term ones that occur weekly, monthly or seasonally?

Routines that occur regularly offer a stable and comfortable
Rhythm in an unpredictable world.

week 6

M

T

W

T

F

S

S

Part Four: Natural Influences

It may seem trivial to talk about the impact of small gestures like filling a vase with flowers, walking on wood flooring or connecting to the outdoors through wide open windows, but it is not. When people and their living spaces are in step with the rhythms of nature, they become connected to the world in a profound way.

"To affect the quality of the day,
that is the highest of arts."

Henry David Thoreau

WEEK 7

Making the Most of Nature:
Inside & Out

One of the easiest paths to Comfort Living is so obvious that, as with Dorothy's efforts to return to Kansas, it is easily overlooked. Nature.

Nature has a way of softening the edges of modern life. It's why we revel in a beach vacation or an escape to the mountains. But who says that you can't enjoy these experiences at home? The urge to stop and smell the roses can become part of daily living when you incorporate natural elements into your surroundings.

Sunlight, cut flowers, plants, wood, stone, natural fibers, animals, breezes... all of these have the power to stabilize and calm. Small but significant elements like these are what keep interiors alive — and believe it or not, they can have that same energizing effect on people.

Every home has access to some form of nature. Whether your outdoor space consists of a park down the street, the view through an apartment window, a small balcony or acres of farmland, there are lots of ways to incorporate the natural world into your Campfires and throughout your home. The great news is that it doesn't have to cost you a cent.

BITS AND PIECES — Bring back Treasures from outdoor moments. Pine cones, feathers, stones, shells — each of these can take on extra meaning when honored on a shelf, tray, mantle or in a vase or basket. Believe it or not, these incidentals can help to offset the pressures of modern life.

FLOWERS — Arrange some cut flowers or greens and place them where they can be enjoyed by all. Whether they come from the grocery store or your backyard, the impact of a branch of forsythia or some daisies in a glass of water is much deeper than you realize.

COLOR — Take color cues from the great outdoors for an ideal Bridge to nature. Consider sky, water and earth and stone colors — but don't forget the vibrant orange of a tangerine, the tawny gold of honey or the delicate lavender of lilacs. What are the colors that speak to you?

BUILDING MATERIALS — Incorporate all-natural materials into your living spaces — options include flooring, countertops, tile, carpeting, cabinetry, upholstered furniture and window treatments.

ACCENTS — Keep an eye out for accents that can bring some nature into your home such as wooden boxes, woven place mats, cotton napkins, baskets, wooden hooks, picture frames and natural-fiber rugs.

FABRICS AND SOFT FURNISHINGS — The way a sofa or armchair feels matters a lot more than how it looks from the doorway. Soft, textured fabrics like corduroy, microsuede, chenille and velvet are so inviting. Natural fibers like linen, silk and even burlap have their own unique character and are great options for throw pillows, window treatments or even entire walls.

COOKING — Buy your herbs as live plants, soil and all. Plant them in window boxes or containers just outside your kitchen so that taking a few steps to cut rosemary or oregano becomes a quick nature break. When the weather cools off, relocate them to a wintertime resting place on a kitchen windowsill.

FRESH AIR — On a nice day, open those windows w-i-d-e. Not only will you and your home be reinvigorated, but you will have created a Bridge to bring the outdoors even closer. At night, just cracking the window allows for yet another easy connection with the outdoors.

WINDOWS — There's no rule that says that windows require draperies. Make the most of a view by eliminating unnecessary curtains or shades and clean the glass to allow all the light to come through. Think about using French doors instead of smaller windows to bring nature even closer.

My ToolBox for Nature

FOUND OBJECTS / shells, stones, feathers

PLANTS / trees, shrubs, flowers, herbs, vegetable and cutting gardens

NATURAL ACCENTS / baskets, placemats, napkin rings, wooden bowls, chopping blocks

BRIDGES TO OUTDOORS / windows, views, French and sliding doors with glass panels, screens, balconies, walkways

LIGHT / sunlight, candlelight, firelight, gas light, outdoor lighting

COLOR / hues taken from nature

BUILDING MATERIALS / wood, stone, natural fibers

OUTDOOR ROOMS / balconies, terraces, patios, tree houses, courtyards, gazebos, pool houses, barbeque areas

SHADE / awnings, umbrellas, trellises, arbors, trees

CONTAINERS / window boxes, planting containers, flower pots, vases, flea market finds, compost heaps

WATER / fountains, water features, bird feeders, garden hoses, irrigation systems

OUTDOOR ROOMS — Energize balconies, terraces and porches with wicker or teak chairs, colorful cushions and a market umbrella or awning for an irresistible outdoor Campfire. Whether you are indoors or out, exterior lighting brings life to outdoor spaces. With candles, matches and something to keep the bugs away, rocking chairs will continue rocking until well after the sun goes down.

LANDSCAPING — Blur the lines between man-made structures and nature with well-chosen landscaping. A nondescript wall blanketed in Boston ivy or Confederate jasmine is enchanting. A wrought-iron arbor or picket fence covered in New Dawn roses is such a pleasure.

Week Seven / To Do's

It's time to venture out and see what you can bring back to your nest. Find what you love and make nature your partner in Comfort Living!

ACTIONS

- Today buy 2 bunches of flowers and, along with any cuttings from outside, make at least 3 arrangements for different areas of your home. Hint: A single flower on a dinner tray or entry table counts!
- Schedule your daily sessions to bring nature into at least 3 areas of your home — indoors and out. Think about adding nature to your existing Campfires.
- Create or improve on 3 nature routines that are meaningful to you — and then put them into practice. They could be as simple as using honey with your tea or sleeping with the window open.

OBSERVATIONS

- How do you feel in your home as a result of your nature changes?

- What are your nature plans for next week? Next month?

Nature has the power to soothe and inspire without costing you a cent.

week 7

M

T

W

T

F

S

S

WEEK 8

Changing with the Times:
Nature as Your Guide

Nature is always in the process of change. Daily, weekly, seasonally. The sun moves across the sky, the days are overcast or warm with sunshine, tides rise and fall, leaves fall to the ground and new ones take their place ... Shifts like these can also become gentle reminders for change and growth in your own life.

For some reason, when it comes to the way we dress, change just happens. When it rains, we carry an umbrella; when it gets cold, out come the sweaters and coats; in spring, playful colors and patterns are everywhere. Granted, our instincts are influenced by the worlds of fashion and retailing, but Mother Nature is leading the way.

So why not trust nature to be our guide in our living spaces as well?

Why aren't modern homes followers of these gentle cycles of nature? With the exception of seasonal thermostat adjustments and holidays when homes are decked out in their finery, modern-day homes are static and inflexible. Homes are built to withstand the elements, but in the process, they block out some of the treats that nature has to offer.

Imagine a three-way conversation between nature, your physical surroundings and yourself. Nature would be like an old friend coming over, whose opinions would be welcomed and respected. There would be a give and take. For example, the response to gorgeous weather might be to open all the windows and enjoy time on the porch. On a cold and nasty weekend, the likely response would be to spend the day cocooning in front of the fireplace reading magazines or watching movies. Though these are simple and predictable actions, it is easy to become so preoccupied that we don't even register what is happening outside. Instead, we crank up the air conditioning or heating and remain oblivious to the deeper Rhythms of nature.

Farm to Table

Buy, prepare and eat foods that are in season, whether they are organic, locally grown or not. This is one of the most immediate ways to tap into natural influences. The farm-to-table mindset appears to be back for good, and experimenting with seasonal offerings is a perfect link to the present.

Animals

Put up a bird feeder, fountain or birdbath outside a window as a way station in winter. Speaking of animals, there's nothing like seeing a cat curled up on a window seat or taking your dog out for a walk.

More on Bits and Pieces

By the time winter comes around, that bowl of shells might be ready for some time off. How about substituting some nuts or pine cones and, while you're at it, putting some logs in the fireplace? Go for a walk, and there's no telling what you will bring home!

More on Color

Changing colors in your home makes for instant gratification — and it doesn't mean painting entire rooms. In the colder months, accents in rich colors like camel, chocolate, and deep reds make homes feel cozy and secure. When the weather warms up, whites, creams, brights and pales can take their place, conveying the more casual spirit of the season. In early spring, fuschia, celery green or pale lavender candles totally renew a dining room and living room.

More on Accents

In addition to color changes, another easy way to fall in step with nature is by bringing seasonally focused elements out of hiding, while retiring others for a well-deserved break. Swapping out throw pillows, placemats, hand towels or just the pillow cases on your bed can reinvigorate spaces. Need inspiration? Check out current issues of home magazines and catalogues as well as stores and websites. An excursion to a flea market is a great place for one-of-a-kind, of-the-moment finds.

The power of nature is ripe for the picking — all you have to do is reach for it!

SLIPCOVERS
A Tried-and-True Routine

Slipcovers are part of a home ritual that has been making a comeback in recent years. This seasonal transition begins with spring cleaning and is capped off with lightweight slipcovers that move darker fabrics and heavier textures into the background for the warmer months. While these easy-going linens and cottons top off upholstered furnishings, light-hearted accents find their way onto tabletops and fireplace mantles as well as other areas of a home. The result is a bit of whimsy and fun — a welcome change from the cold winter months. Then, when the summer draws to a close, those same slipcovers are sent back into hibernation until the following spring.

Week Eight / To Do's

Begin your dialogue with the Rhythms of nature. Keep in mind *when* you are, not just *where* you are.

ACTIONS

- Get outside today! Absorb what's happening around you. Scribble a few notes to yourself, and bring some of nature home with you. Incorporate these bits and pieces into your home Campfires and routines.

- Schedule your sessions for the rest of the week, and continue your dialogue with nature. Take time to listen to the Rhythms around you. Use nature's cues to enrich your Campfires or routines. For example, if the weather is growing colder, place a throw blanket within easy reach — and use it. If spring is approaching and daylight hours are getting longer, relocate your daily cup of tea or mail-reading session to a spot where you can absorb the sun's warmth.

- Try your hand at building some simple Bridges to nature. Some ideas: open some windows, move a chair for a better view, change your screen saver, make a shopping list of produce in season.

- As you near the end of the week, take time to add to your Personal Profile on pages 74 and 75.

OBSERVATIONS

- In allowing yourself to be guided by nature, what changes do you feel in your home?

- Do you feel a change in yourself? Do you feel the pace of your life shifting? What seems to be working?

> Nature can be a trusted and essential tool for encouraging a more comfortable stride in fast-paced times.

week 8

M

T

W

T

F

S

S

Afterword

"Treat each other as you would an honored guest."

A Chinese wedding wish

Last, But Not Least

If a plant receives light and water, it will thrive — and possibly offer a flower in return. If that plant is ignored, it will wither away. In any relationship, the back-and-forth is key. When there is respect and care flowing in both directions, there is comfort, meaning, community and growth.

These 4 characters are traditionally offered to newlyweds in China.
Their translation is quoted on the opposite page.

While this blessing is intended for couples, the same holds true for the relationships that each of us has with our homes. When we honor our surroundings and treat our homes with respect, love and care, the favor will be returned many times over.

Terms

Balance
A way of living in harmony with the outside world. Balance is achieved by being aware of change and flexible to make adjustments along the way.

Bridges
People, places, objects and routines that ease connection and flow.

Campfires
Easy but intentional combinations of objects and routines that draw people in for a sense of well-being, comfort and community.

Comfort Home Words
The words that describe how a home ideally should feel to the people who live there.

Comfort Living
A lifestyle that emphasizes inner priorities and meaningful experiences.

Echo
A type of Bridge that connects the present to the past, by associating deeper meanings to ordinary objects.

Lifestyle Design
The intentional process of using Campfires and practical tools to create a life that encourages balance, ease and quality of life.

Lifestyle Priorities
The critical needs and wants of an individual's life.
Top Treasures + Comfort Home Words = Lifestyle Priorities

Obstacles
Anything or anyone that gets in the way of positive experiences.

Rhythm
The unique pace of a person's life, based on inner priorities and outward routines.

ToolBox
A list of people, places and things that can be used as a means to creating and living a Comfort Life.

Treasures
Experiences, people, places and objects that are personally meaningful and encourage happiness, contentment, connection or joy.

Streamlining
The 4-phase process of making the most of positives and the least of negatives in a person's life: Preserve/Honor, Put Away/Store, Give Away/Sell and Recycle/Throw Away.

An Invitation to Connect

"We shape our dwellings, and afterwards,
our dwellings shape us."

Sir Winston Churchill

I hope your journey with *Comfort Living* has been enjoyable and worthwhile. Please stay connected and share your stories, thoughts, successes and stumbling blocks as you continue on your path to a more balanced lifestyle.

Meanwhile, here are 3 quick questions for you:

1. Has *Comfort Living* changed the way you think about your life and home?

2. What 3 words would describe your experience with this book?

3. Would you recommend *Comfort Living* to a friend, colleague or client? (Please do, by the way!)

Stay Connected

Contact us about presentations for upcoming meetings or special events. Here's how:

Website: comfortlivingbychristine.com for blogs, upcoming events, orders and
          our quarterly e-communication.
E-mail: comments@comfortlivingbychristine.com
Twitter: @comfort_living
Mail: Christine Eisner, P.O. Box 52107, Atlanta, GA 30355

My Profile

My Personal ToolBox

People Tools

_____   _____   _____

_____   _____   _____

_____   _____   _____

Place Tools

_____   _____   _____

_____   _____   _____

_____   _____   _____

Thing Tools

_____   _____   _____

_____   _____   _____

_____   _____   _____

My Profile

Activity	Daily	Weekly/Monthly	Other
My Routines			
Streamlining			
Campfire Creation			
Campfire Tending			
Bridge Building			
Echo Formation			
Nature Connection			

My Profile

My Name _____ Date _____

My Top Treasures:

_____   _____   _____

_____   _____   _____

_____   _____   _____

My Biggest Obstacles:

_____   _____   _____

_____   _____   _____

My Top Comfort Words:

_____   _____   _____

_____   _____   _____

My Lifestyle Priorities:

_____

_____

My Areas to Streamline:

_____

_____

My Profile

My Campfires:

_____   _____   _____

_____   _____   _____

My Bridges:

_____   _____   _____

_____   _____   _____

My Echoes:

_____   _____   _____

_____   _____   _____

My Top Comfort Living Routines:

_____   _____   _____

_____   _____   _____

My Rhythms:

_____   _____   _____

_____   _____   _____

My Natural Influences:

_____   _____   _____

_____   _____   _____

Notes

Acknowledgements

Comfort Living is dedicated with love to my mother Annette Leuthold, and to my father and stepmother, Dolph and Nhumy Leuthold. I am so fortunate to have been shaped by your views and values over the years. Without your combined influences, this book would not have been possible.

Life is a journey and to my own surprise, *Comfort Living* has now become part of mine. Writing and producing a book is by no means an overnight process, nor is it a solo effort. So of course, I have a number of very special people to thank:

Janice Shay, you were my guardian angel in producing and designing this book; and Paula Schwed, your talents as an editor and guide were invaluable. The two of you immediately understood what I was trying to convey and managed to bring this book even farther than I dreamed possible. Ditto for Amy Collins MacGregor. Here's to a future endeavor! To John Waluskiewicz, from the Savannah College of Art & Design, thank you for the hours spent on visuals. To Chris Cann and Erica Hartfield, I could not have pulled this off without your enthusiasm and behind-the-scenes support. Thanks too, to Christine Fisher and Allison Lambert, for your assistance in prior years.

I appreciate the generosity of such very talented photographers, as well as the words of individuals who so graciously offered testimonials on my behalf. Also to Carol Mann, Herb Meyer and Bert Russo, thank you for your continued interest and support of my work.

To Denise Miller, Danica Kombol, Jack Cassidy and Dana Sanderson, there just aren't words that express how much you each mean to me. To so many others who enrich my life in all sorts of ways, among them: Genevieve Bos, Joyce Caldwell, Vladimir Chubinsky, Tony Conway, Donna Cooper, Harriet and Murray Eisner, John Goodwin, Betty and Billy Hulse, Anmy Leuthold and Mick Breitenstein, Jax Peters Lowell, Wendy Palmer Patterson, Carlyle Rollins, Margaret Russell, Frances Schultz, Betsy Sechrest, Janece Shaffer, Clint Smith, Linda Tarkenton, Helen Weeks and Kristen Worthe. Thank you also to my book club, my Gr-8 ladies, my riding and tennis buddies, and to the Women that Cook. The experiences I share with you are among my Treasures.

And finally, to my husband, Dean, and our two children, Matthew and Sarah, you have been the inspiration for me to enrich our life at home. Matthew and Sarah, I love you not only as my children, but also for the individuals that you are. Dean, I learn from you every day and thank you from the bottom of my heart for your support and encouragement of this book and in our life together. Here's to our past, present — and future.

Praise for *Comfort Living*

Accessible, practical, and possible, Christine Eisner's Comfort Living *offers wisdom and inspiration for us all. Dispensed in a step-by-step format, her inquiries and exercises really make us think about the everyday elements of how and where we live, and how easy it can be to transform our homes — and our lives — for the better.*
— Frances Schultz, Contributing Editor for House Beautiful magazine, former co-host of
"Southern Living Presents" and author of Atlanta at Table and Atlanta at Home

Christine Eisner begins with the fundamental insight that our homes can shape our lives, and follows up with a series of insightful ideas and questions. The result is not just a book on home design, but a guide to living a more satisfying life. Comfort Living *shows us how to find ways to make our homes support the ways we really want to live.*
— Charles Brewer, Founder of MindSpring and developer of the new town of Las Catalinas, Costa Rica
and the award-winning Glenwood Park neighborhood

Comfort Living *represents an outline to restore America's social web-work. This phenomenal diagram will allow American families to once again create a home life that will instill values in our children while nurturing them to understand that home is a refuge of life where love and safety reside. What comes to mind is a great saying by Abraham Lincoln, "The strength of a nation lives in the homes of it's people."*
— Ralph Avallone, President, National Green Energy Council

Today, we see a value shift happening in the world. People are seeking out what truly makes them happy, from how and what they eat, to their friends and community, to the space they live in. Christine Eisner's book can serve as a sort of manual for this process, by encouraging people to step off the treadmill of life, look inward, and determine what's truly important to them.
— Steve Nygren, Founder of Serenbe

Look out Martha Stewart! In these highly stressful times, Comfort Living, *Christine Eisner's new book, strikes just the right balance. Eisner's accessible style inspires each of us to find balance and harmony in our immediate natural surroundings. And for those of us wanting more grace and energy in our lives,* Comfort Living *is a must read.*
— Anne Kreamer, author of Going Gray — What I Learned About Beauty, Sex, Work,
Motherhood, Authenticity and Everything Else that Matters

Christine Eisner presents many of the principles of modern living — how one's environment shapes lifestyle, how to integrate the discipline of order with the soulfulness of displaying treasured objects, and even an approach to designing space by evaluating daily routines. Rarely do you find a guide which breaks down the process of creating a "home" versus just a "house."
— Christy MacLear, Executive Director, The Philip Johnson Glass House, National Trust for Historic Preservation

Comfort Living *empowers us to elevate pedestrian living spaces into something magical and meaningful. Throughout the book, Christine Eisner displays a rare gift for teaching others how to create a transcendent experience with good design.* Comfort Living *is simply a joy to read.*
— Paula S. Wallace, President, Savannah College of Art and Design and co-author of *A House in the South*

Christine Eisner is a modern-day alchemist. She deconstructs the everyday, and allows you to re-imagine what is possible within the confines of today's busy, frenetic lifestyles. With an ample dose of wisdom and a dash of wit, Comfort Living *is a veritable prescription to making the most of every moment — and having every moment have meaning. Eisner's unparalleled insight provides guidance, support and, most importantly, inspiration for those seeking a more balanced way of living.*
— Clinton Smith, Editorial Director, *Atlanta Homes & Lifestyles* magazine

I am inspired! When she clicks the heels of her "ruby slippers," designer Christine Eisner transports you to a calmer, clutter-free comfort lifestyle.
— Helen Ballard Weeks, founder of Ballard Designs

Finally! A practical, inspirational home guide for those with little time to organize. A worthy journey that will enrich your living style.
— Elizabeth Franklin, author of *The Franklin Report, The Insider's Guide to the Home*

Full of wisdom and concrete exercises to enhance your well-being by using what is closest at hand: your home. A lovely and inspiring book.
— Harville Hendrix, Ph. D., author of *Getting the Love You Want: A Guide for Couples*

At last, a decorating book that gives us, not the newest designer décor, but lights a path to our own front doors. Christine Eisner's Comfort Living *satisfies a deep-down hunger for beautiful surroundings, connection, ease. Like a good friend with an uncanny eye for the personal detail, she draws around us a warm circle of light, shows us the way to create a shelter from the storm of modern life.*
— Jax Peters Lowell, author of *The Gluten-Free Bible,* and a novel, *Mothers*

Christine has a remarkable ability to incorporate antique and vintage pieces into living spaces, naturally and easily. Objects that "have been steeped in their own juices" will both put a smile on any homeowner's face and add character and life to their living environments.
— Mark Sage, owner, Love Train Antiques and BoBo Intriguing Objects

More Comfort Living

Now that your journey has begun, we hope you will share this guide with others. To order additional copies, visit our website at www.comfortlivingbychristine.com, call 800.345.6665 or complete the form below:

Comfort Living: A Back-to-Basics Guide to a More Balanced Lifestyle
$19.95 each + $5 shipping and handling for the first book (add $2 for each additional book when all are shipped to the same address)

The Comfort Living Journal
A spiral-bound companion booklet for recording Treasures, Obstacles, thoughts, resolutions and To Do's. $7.95 each + $4 shipping and handling (add $1 shipping for each additional book when shipped to the same address)

Buy 2 or more copies of the book, and receive one complimentary copy of the journal. (Limit one per mailing address.) To inquire about quantity discounts or special orders, e-mail us at: info@comfortlivingbychristine.com or call 404.365.8317.

Please send me _____ copies of *Comfort Living* and _____ copies of *The Comfort Living Journal*. Enclosed is a total of $_____ , which includes shipping and handling. Georgia residents only, add 8% tax.

Complete this form or pay online at www.comfortlivingbychristine.com

☐ credit card # (Mastercard, Visa, Discover): _____ exp: _____

signature: _____ date: _____ CVV # _____
(on back of card)

☐ check   (payable to **Pathway Book Service**)   ☐ money order

Ship To:

name: _____

street: _____

city/state/zip: _____

e-mail: _____ tel: _____

Please return this form with your payment to:

PBS — Comfort Living
P.O. Box 89
Gilsum, NH 03448
phone: 800.345.6665
fax: 603.357.2073

LIFESTYLE DESIGN

Copyright © 2009

ISBN# 978-0-9842282-0-1

Production and Design by Pinafore Press / Janice Shay

Photography by:

Marcy J. Levinson-Brooks, courtesy of *The Atlanta Jewish Times*: 43

Brownlow & Sons: 53

Christine Eisner: 2 (Athens exterior, orchid, Bryn Mawr exterior, Atlanta entry, Florida pool), 3 (Kenya vanity, Charleston window box, Useppa exterior, Kenya sitting area, Tybee light house) 11(Woodstock entry), 14, 23 (South Beach seating area), 59, 65, 72

Dean Eisner: 84

Oberto Gili: 2 (NYC apartment)

The Print Shop: Cover, 6, 12, 28, 39 (glassware, wine opener), 42, 52, 64 (steps)

Tina Rowden: 3 (red pillows), 15, 39 (candles, sushi tray), 58

Natalie Thavenot: 2 (lamp), 11 (countertop), 64 (side table)

John Waluskiewicz: 2 (landing, breezeway), 3 (carousel horse, lamp, side table), 4, 8, 11 (den), 19, 23 (mantle, vanity), 31, 34, 36, 39 (frames, shelves, settee, rocker, guitar), 44, 47, 51, 56, 63, 69

Printed in Canada

For information:

LIFESTYLE DESIGN
P.O. Box 52107
Atlanta, GA 30355
www.comfortlivingbychristine.com